KANGAROOS

KANGAROOS

JENNY MARKERT

THE CHILD'S WORLD

DESIGN
Bill Foster of Albarella & Associates, Inc.

PHOTO CREDITS
Len Rue Jr.: front cover, back cover, 23
Leonard Rue III: 6, 25
Frank Todd/Ecosystems International: 2, 15, 29
COMSTOCK/Hartman-DeWitt: 8, 11, 12
COMSTOCK/Phylis Greenberg: 19, 20
COMSTOCK/Georg Gerster: 27
The Zoological Society of San Diego: 16
Ralph A. Clevenger: 30

Distributed to schools and libraries
in Canada by
SAUNDERS BOOK CO.
Collingwood, Ontario, Canada L9Y 3Z7
(800) 461-9120

Library of Congress Cataloging-in-Publication Data
Markert, Jenny.
Kangaroos/Jenny Markert.
p. cm. — (Child's World Wildlife Library)
Summary: Describes the characteristics and behavior
of the kangaroo.
ISBN 0-89565-715-5
1. Kangaroos — Juvenile literature.   [1. Kangaroos.]   I. Title.
II. Series.   91-13374
QL737.M35M27 1991   CIP
599.2—dc20   AC

For Nancy

As the sun rises over the grassy plains of Australia, kangaroos hop out to greet it. The night has been cool, and the animals are eager for the sun's warmth. It is September, springtime in Australia. Many of the female kangaroos, called *does*, are ready to give birth.

Glancing over her shoulder, a female kangaroo retreats to the shade of a nearby tree. Unlike male kangaroos, the doe has a special sack on her belly called a *pouch*. She licks her pouch to make it clean and soft for the arrival of her young. Using her powerful hind legs, the doe digs a small hole in the ground. Then she sits down and gives birth to a little baby kangaroo.

The newborn kangaroo, called a *joey*, is about the size of a peanut M&M! It is blind, hairless, and not yet ready for life on its own. The joey crawls up its mother's stomach and into her warm, cozy pouch. In the pouch, the joey grabs hold of one of its mother's nipples, or *teats*. The teats give the joey special milk that helps it grow.

About 5 months later, as summer gives way to autumn, the joey peeks out of the pouch and takes its first look at the world. It is no longer blind or hairless. It is covered with soft, brown fur.

Soon the joey pushes itself all the way out of the pouch. Testing its new legs, the joey hops along behind its mother. When danger is near, the joey leaps headfirst into its mother's pouch. Then it does a somersault and peeks out to see the commotion. Though the joey also retreats to its mother's pouch for an occasional sip of milk, it begins to eat grass and leaves like the grown-up kangaroos.

When the joey is about 8 months old, its mother gives birth to another baby kangaroo. The first joey, now called a *young-at-heel*, can no longer seek shelter in its mother's pouch. There is not enough room for both it and the new joey. Fortunately, the young-at-heel needs its mother less and less. It eats more grass and less milk now. When it is about a year and a half old, it can survive on its own.

To most people, a kangaroo is a kangaroo. However, not all kangaroos are alike. There are 58 different kinds, or *species*, of kangaroos. They come in a wide variety of sizes. The smallest kangaroo, the rat kangaroo, grows only as big as a squirrel. The red kangaroo, on the other hand, can grow as tall as a professional basketball player. With its muscular back legs, an adult red kangaroo can leap over the top of a school bus — the long way!

Wild kangaroos live only in Australia. Many inhabit Australia's grassy plains and dry riverbeds. Others prefer rocky hills or forests. The tree kangaroo is a forest dweller that can scramble up a tree when it is scared! Another unusual kangaroo, called a burrowing boodie, lives underground.

All kangaroos are vegetarians. They eat only plants. Kangaroos that live in the forests eat tree leaves and shrubs. Kangaroos that live in the open plains prefer to eat grass.

Kangaroos often eat and drink in big groups called *mobs*. Mobs, which can contain more than 100 kangaroos, provide safety for the young and old kangaroos. If danger is near, male kangaroos, called *boomers*, make loud thumping noises with their feet as they hop away to safety. This thumping warns the other mob members of danger. Then all the kangaroos scatter.

If a kangaroo is unable to escape from an enemy, it is not defenseless. The threatened kangaroo leans back on its tail and kicks the enemy with its powerful back legs. Kangaroos have a big, middle toenail on their back feet that can inflict a painful scratch. They also use their front arms to box an enemy. Sometimes kangaroos box with each other just for fun!

Kangaroos have many enemies in the wild. Pythons, wild pigs, cats, and eagles all prey on young kangaroos and joeys. The kangaroo's worst enemy, however, is the Australian wild dog, or *dingo*. Dingoes often roam across the Australian grasslands in large packs. They will attack joeys, does, and even boomers. An adult kangaroo can defend itself against a single dingo but is no match for a pack of wild dogs.

Humans are another enemy of the kangaroo. When settlers first moved to Australia, wild kangaroos destroyed many of their crops. In order to protect their fields, people poisoned and shot thousands of kangaroos. Today, people are still a threat to kangaroos. Humankind has developed many areas where kangaroos used to roam free. People also kill kangaroos to make pet food or to use their hides for clothing. Along with these hazards, hundreds of kangaroos are hit by cars each year.

Despite all these dangers, kangaroos continue to thrive. The Australian government has created national parks and preserves where kangaroos can live undisturbed by humans. So, as the sun sinks below Australia's grassy plains, kangaroos can still find safety. They rest peacefully under a tree or behind a bush, awaiting the warmth of another day.